Wendy On \
Goes to the Zoo

By Angela Ruzicka

Illustrated by Elizabeth Gearhart

The character Brandon, featured in this book, is named after Brandon O'Harver from De Soto, Missouri. Brandon was diagnosed with Duchenne Muscular Dystrophy at the age of four. In 2006, he began to use a wheelchair full-time. He enjoys a wide range of activities, such as camping and anything else outdoors. Like Brandon in the book, he is very interested in insects and takes many in from his grandmother's yard. Though this disease weakens his muscles, Brandon has never felt weak. He still dreams of being a police officer when he grows up.

Brandon embodies the attitude I portray with the Wendy on Wheels series. In honor of Brandon, a portion of the profits of this book will be donated to the Muscular Dystrophy Association.

I hope you enjoy *Wendy on Wheels Goes to the Zoo*. As always, please feel free to email me with any comments, questions, or ideas.

Thank you!

Angela Ruzicka

angela@wendyonwheels.com

Wendy On Wheels
Goes to the Zoo

By Angela Ruzicka
Illustrated by Elizabeth Gearhart

To Selah,
I hope you enjoy
Wendy's trip to the
zoo.
Best Wishes,
Angela Ruzicka

Published by Angela Ruzicka
www.wendyonwheels.com
ISBN 978-0-615-39787-0

Thank you, Mom and Dad, for all you have done for me.

Thanks to the St. Louis Zoo, for being my backdrop
for this book. For the record, The Primate House has been
accessible since the late 1970s.

Thanks, Aunt Elaine, for your help with
the discussion questions.

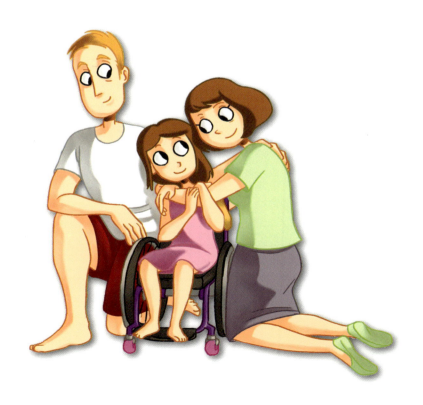

One day, Wendy's teacher, Mrs. Nealy took the class on a field trip to the zoo. Wendy felt very excited. She couldn't wait to see the monkeys, her favorite animal.

A zoo guide met the class when they arrived inside.

First stop on the tour was the Asian elephants.
Wendy wheeled next to her friend, Michelle.

Next on the tour was the cheetah, who lay asleep in the grass.
Wendy's friend, Brandon rolled closely behind her.

The guide told the class about the red river hog. "You will notice the Red River Hog has a white ring around his eye," he said. Wendy felt anxious. "Mrs. Nealy, when are we going to see the monkeys?" "Calm down, Wendy," Mrs. Nealy said. "We will see the primate house after lunch."

Next, the class saw some meerkats. Wendy loved the meerkats.

After the meerkats, it was time for lunch. Wendy took off her gloves and cleaned her hands with a moist wipe before she ate.

Wendy and her friends enjoyed lunch while
watching the birds in the lake.

As the class climbed the steps to the primate house, Mrs. Nealy
noticed there was no way to get Wendy and Brandon inside.

"You two will have to wait right here," She said. "It will just be about five minutes, then we will see something else." With that, Mrs. Nealy walked up the stairs and entered the primate house.

"That's not fair!!! I've been waiting to see monkeys all day," Wendy cried.
Brandon agreed, "That's not right!!!"

Wendy got an idea. "We passed the chimpanzee area back there. Let's go back and see them."

"I don't know if we should," Brandon said nervously.
"As long as we are back in five minutes, Mrs. Nealy won't know we
were gone," Wendy explained. "Come on, Brandon, let's roll!"

Wendy felt giddy as the two entered the chimpanzee habitat. They saw several chimps walking across the grass.

Two chimpanzees walked up to the glass. Wendy took
out her camera and snapped a quick picture of her and Brandon with
their new chimpanzee friends.

Wendy and Brandon laughed as the chimps made
funny faces at them.

As they exited the habitat, Brandon saw the insectarium.
"We have to go in there!"
Wendy figured they could sneak back in with the class shortly after.
"Let's go!"

Brandon and Wendy saw some spiders and
scorpions in the insectarium.

Next door to the insectarium was the butterfly house. The two watched carefully where they rolled so they wouldn't hurt the butterflies.

They saw beautiful butterflies. One landed on Wendy's shirt.

Brandon laughed as a butterfly landed on the back of his wheelchair.
They were having a wonderful time.

Meanwhile, back at the front of the zoo,
Mrs. Nealy and the class waited nervously.

"Where are Brandon and Wendy?"
She and the zoo workers had been searching all over the zoo
since the class left the primate house.
"WENDY!!! BRANDON!!!" Wendy and Brandon's parents had been
called and were on their way to the zoo to find them.

Wendy and Brandon were in the penguin area.
Wendy loved seeing the cute penguins.

Brandon enjoyed watching the penguins jump in and out of the water.

The polar bears were right outside the exit of the penguin area, so Wendy and Brandon took pictures of a polar bear.

Wendy said, "We should probably go find the class now, Brandon.
Hopefully, nobody has noticed we've been gone."

They followed the path around to the front of the zoo.

"Brandon! Wendy!" The class shouted, as the saw them.

Wendy's mom, dad, and sister ran to meet Wendy .
"Wendy, we were worried about you," her mom said.
"I'm sorry, Mom." Wendy responded. "I just wanted to see the primates,
and when we couldn't go in, we decided to see the chimps instead."

Mrs. Nealy was angry. "You were both asked to wait right outside!"

Wendy's dad spoke up. "Now wait a minute, Mrs. Nealy. You took the rest of the class into the monkey house and left them outside? All Wendy wanted was to do what the rest of the class got to do. Wendy and Brandon are members of your class too.

If your class activity can't include everybody, then
you need to rearrange the activity."
Mrs. Nealy thought about what he said. "You are right. I guess I should
have called the zoo ahead of time and made sure the whole class could
be part of the whole tour. I'm sorry, Wendy. I'm sorry, Brandon."

"I know it wasn't fair that you were left out," Wendy's mom said. "But you should really listen to your teacher, Wendy. We were worried about you."
"I'm sorry, Mom and Dad," Wendy said. "Sorry, Mrs. Nealy."
"Yeah sorry, Mrs. Nealy," Brandon said quietly.

Mrs. Nealy smiled. "That's okay. Now we know for next time."

It was the end of the day and the class got back on the bus. Wendy waved goodbye to her friends and went home with her family. She yawned. It had been an exciting, yet tiring day.

Discussion Questions

1. How would you feel if you were left out of an activity with your class because of something you had no control over?

2. Do you think it was fair that Mrs. Nealy asked Wendy and Brandon to wait outside?

3. What could the zoo have done to make sure the whole class could participate?

4. What could Mrs. Nealy have done to include Wendy and Brandon?

5. What could Wendy and Brandon have done differently?

THE END!!!

LaVergne, TN USA
11 October 2010
200367LV00002BA